Ist BATTALION SCOTS GUARDS

WEST BELFAST

May - November 1992

edited by Lt Col T.S.Spicer SG

First published 1993

Published by Owl Press PO Box 315 Downton, Salisbury, Wiltshire SP5 3YE.
Printed and bound in Great Britain by J H Haynes & Co Ltd Sparkford,
Nr. Yeovil, Somerset.
Origination and design by Owl Press.

British Library Cataloguing-in-Publication Data. A catalogue record for this
book is available from the British Library.
ISBN 0 9515917 9 7

INTRODUCTION

by the Commanding Officer

This book is a photographic record of the work carried out by the 1st Battalion Scots Guards between January and November 1992. It shows the Battalion preparing for and carrying out a six month operational tour. The Battalion trained for its tour in West Belfast between January and May. The training was tough and demanding. It was designed to prepare soldiers for one of the most exacting environments in which they will ever have to serve. Soldiering in Northern Ireland is demanding, not in terms of intense combat but rather because of the difficulty of differentiating between the largely innocent population and the enemy - the terrorist. For six months soldiers must endure the ever present threat of a terrorist ambush and the constant fatigue and strain from working long hours at an unrelenting pace.

The tour of the 1st Battalion Scots Guards lasted from May to November. Throughout that time the soldiers had to discipline themselves to be relaxed and polite, yet firm, in their day to day dealings with the population. At the same time they had to remain constantly alert and suspicious, ready to spring into action when attacked by the enemy (which they were frequently). This is a tall order for a young man who has been trained to fight effectively on a battlefield in the high intensity conflict of general war. It is a great credit to the training system and to the soldiers themselves that they were able to make this transition and acquit themselves in a totally professional way within the constraints of the Rule of Law. The same cannot be said of the terrorist.

This book is designed to be a record. It makes no statement, political or otherwise, other than to display the continuing professionalism of the British soldier. In the main, it will be of interest to those who took part but in addition it will be of value as a historical and photographic record.

During the tour the Battalion did well, making considerable inroads into terrorist organisations. This book is dedicated to all those who were there, to our colleagues in other Regiments who supported us, the Parachute Regiment and Argyle & Sutherland Highlanders, to our various Headquarters and to the RUC, but in particular it is dedicated to the memory of Guardsman Shackleton, Guardsman Wason and Private Lee who died on active service with us.

PART I

TRAINING

January - May

PART II

THE TOUR

May - November

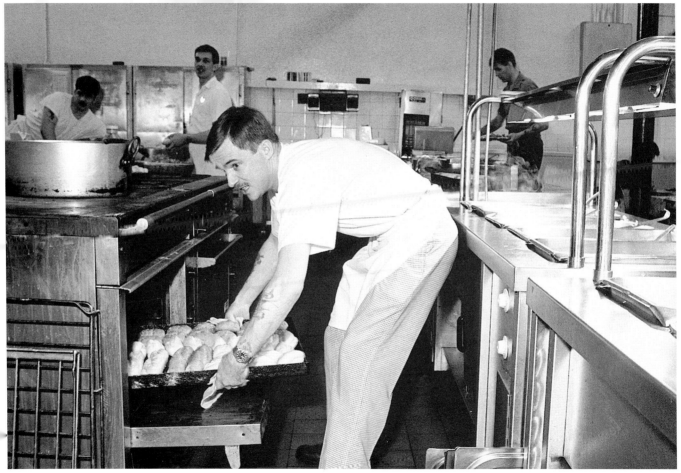

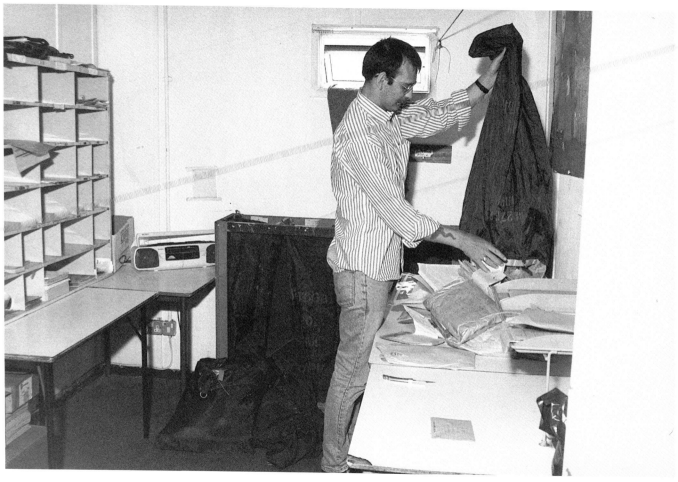

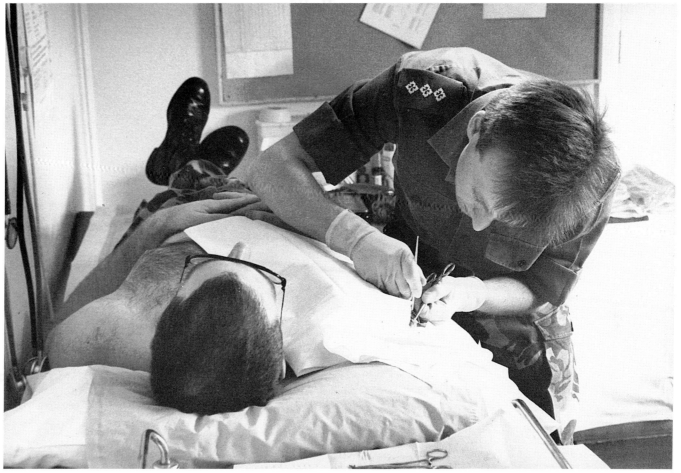

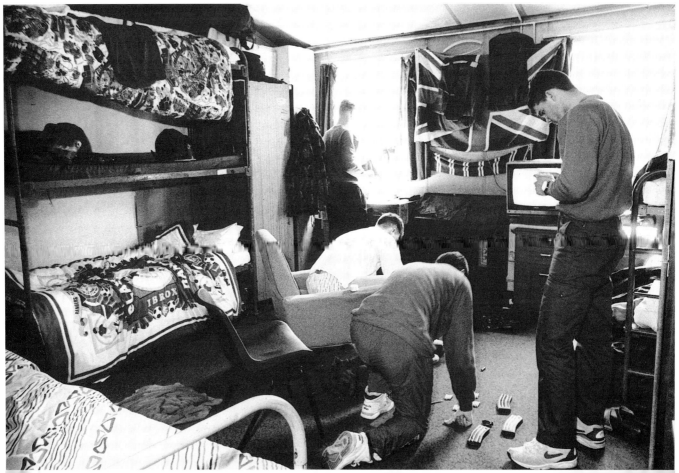

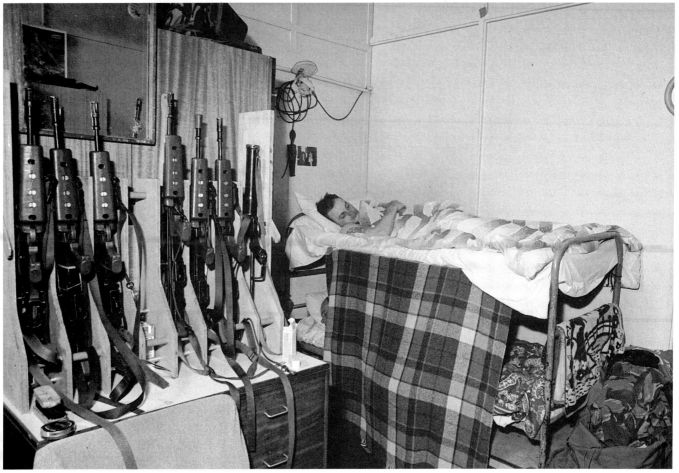

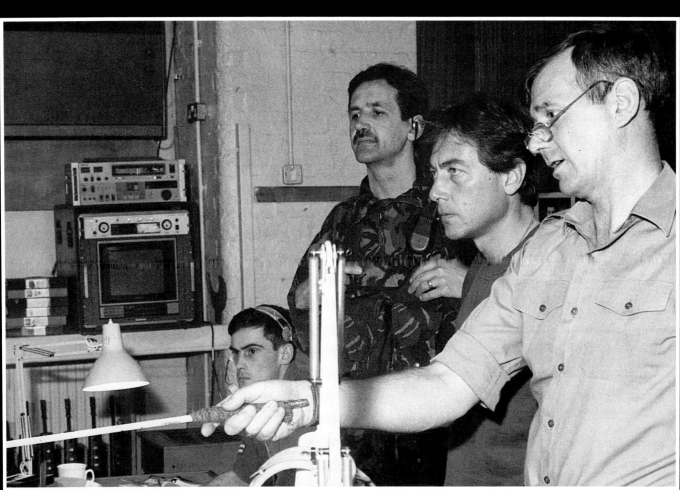

94 KC 25

CONFIDENTIAL TELEPHONE
FREE PHONE
0800 666 999

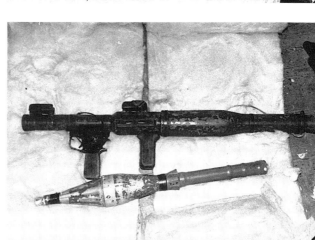

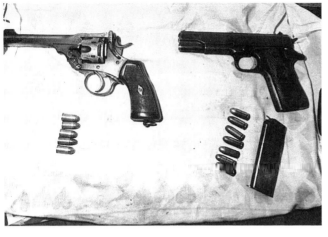

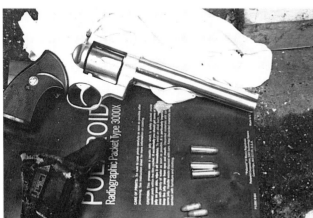
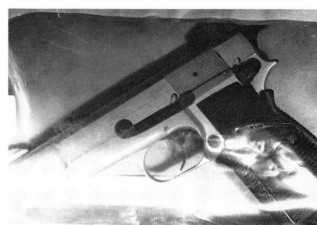

ACKNOWLEDGEMENT TO THE PHOTOGRAPHERS

CSgt John Dadley

Front and back cover photographs.
Pages 30, 31, 32, 33, 34, 35, 36 (RHS), 38, 39 (RHS), 40, 41, 42, 44, 46, 47, 51, 61, 62, 60, 61, 74, 77, 78, 79, 80, 81, 82, 83, 84, 85, 86, 97, 99, 94, 95, 96, 97, 100, 102, 103, 104, 105, 108, 109, 111, 112, 113, 114, 117, 118, 119, 120, 122, 123, 124, 125 and 126.

Miss Rose Bennington

Pages 9, 10, 11, 12, 13, 14, 15, 16, 17, 21, 22, 23, 24, 25, 45, 50, 52, 53, 65, 67, 68, 69, 70, 71, 87, 88, 89, 90, 91, 98, 99, 110 and 116.

Mr Jack Ashton

Pages 26, 27, 28, 29, 36 (LHS), 37, 39 (LHS), 43, 48, 49, 54, 55, 56, 57, 58, 59, 60, 66, 72, 73, 76, 101, 106, 107, 115 and 121.